Contents

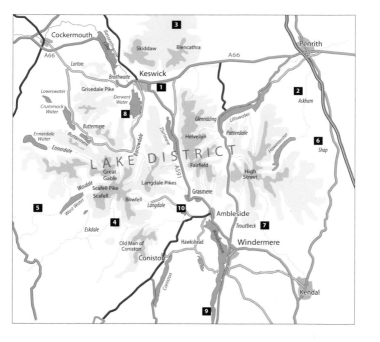

England's Largest National Park

THE LAKE DISTRICT NATIONAL PARK is the largest and most popular of the thirteen National Parks in England and Wales. Created as one of Britain's first National Parks in 1951, its role is to 'conserve and enhance' the natural beauty, wildlife and culture of this iconic English landscape, not just for residents and visitors today but for future generations, too.

Remarkably, the National Park contains every scrap of England's land over 3,000 feet, including its highest mountain, Scafell Pike. Packed within the Park's 885 square miles are numerous peaks and fells, over 400 lakes and tarns, around 50 dales, six National Nature Reserves, and more than 100 Sites of Special Scientific Interest—all publicly accessible on over 1,800 miles of footpaths and other rights of way. It's no surprise then, that the Lake District attracts an estimated 15 million visitors a year.

Castlerigg's Neolithic stone circle against the dramatic backdrop of the Helvellyn range

Lake District history walks

It may not seem obvious at first, but the rich human heritage of the area we now call the Lake District is evident all around us as we walk the fells and dales. From the enigmatic monuments built by prehistoric peoples to the industrial scars left in more modern times, centuries of human habitation have left their mark on this landscape. Keep your eyes and your imagination open, and you will come to realise that every step you take is a step through time.

"And did those feet in ancient time
  Walk upon England's mountains green?"

William Blake, Preface to *Milton*,
now better known as the lyrics to the hymn *Jerusalem*, c.1804

TOP 10 **Walks:** Walks with History

ANCIENT SHIELINGS, BRONZE AGE CAIRNS, Iron Age settlements, industrial archeaology, fortified homes and religious symbols are scattered throughout the Lake District. Much of the area's history remains buried beneath the soil or requires expert interpretation, but the ten walks featured here visit some of the more obvious and dramatic remains. Some of these, particularly the older sites, are found on the low fells, while others are in the valleys, but each involves a superb walk in a landscape that resonates with the memory of former lives.

NEOLITHIC

Castlerigg
Stone Circle

page 8

BRONZE AGE

Moor Divock
stone circle

page 14

IRON AGE

Carrock Fell
hillfort

page 20

ROMAN

Hardknott
Roman fort

page 26

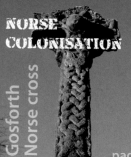

NORSE COLONISATION

Gosforth Norse cross

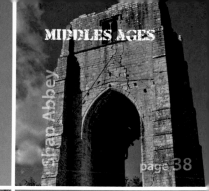

MIDDLES AGES

Shap Abbey

BORDER RAIDS

Kentmere pele tower

ELIZABETHAN

Catbells' mines

INDUSTRIAL REVOLUTION

Stott Park Bobbin Mill

VICTORIAN

Loughrigg Tarn

A dramatic sunset at Castlerigg Stone Circle

Castlerigg Stone Circle

A gentle ramble at the foot of the fells, starting and finishing at an enigmatic prehistoric site

What to expect:
Quiet lanes, low fell, tracks, farm paths, poor signposting

Distance/time: 6.5km/ 4 miles. Allow 2-2½ hours

Start: Roadside parking beside Castlerigg Stone Circle, about 1.5km east of Keswick

Grid ref: GR 291 237

Ordnance Survey Map: Explorer OL 4 The English Lakes *North-western area. Keswick, Cockermouth & Wigton*

After the walk: Horse and Farrier Inn, Thelkeld, near Keswick, Cumbria, CA12 4SQ. www.horseandfarrier.com | 01768779688 | info@horseandfarrier.com

Walk outline

Setting off from the parking area beside Castlerigg Stone Circle—and always within sight of majestic Blencathra—the route uses quiet lanes and farm paths to reach Low Rigg. Passing lonely Tewet Tarn on the way, it climbs up and over this sometimes damp, low-lying fell to the church at St John's in the Vale. From here, a rough track heads downhill and then a series of farm paths are followed back to the stone circle.

Castlerigg Stone Circle

Castlerigg is one of the oldest stone circles in the country, dating back to about 3,000BC, the late Neolithic period. Nobody knows what the people of the New Stone Age would have used it for, although various theories have been put forward over the years. Was it an astronomical observatory? A religious site? Or maybe just a trading centre for hand axes? Today, its functions are many: from photographers' model and tourism attraction to a place of dawn pilgrimage every summer solstice.

Stone shadow

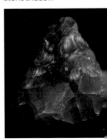

Neolithic flint arrowhead

The Walk

1. From the parking area, head east along the road for about 400 metres. You pass a group of buildings belonging to **Keswick Climbing Wall and Activity Centre** on your left. When you draw level with the white farmhouse in this group, turn right through a gate with a fingerpost beside it. Heading generally east, you now cross a series of fields via gates.

2. When you reach the next road, turn right. At the T-junction, turn right and, almost 300 metres later, right again along a quiet road—signposted 'St John's In The Vale church'.

3. About 350 metres along this road, turn right through a gate with a fingerpost beside it. A faint, grassy track winds its way up through the enclosure and then out through a gap in the top wall.

The way ahead isn't obvious. Head to the waist-high fingerpost about 80 metres to your right. Then, as indicated, bear left (south) to go through a stile about 30 metres up from the edge of **Tewet Tarn**. Head slightly right to pick up a grassy path beside the tarn. Cross a stile next to a large gate. When the wall up to your right swings away, continue along the faint track (south)—crossing damp ground and then climbing slightly. After the next wall stile, keep straight ahead on the broad, grassy track. As you approach the buildings, the track appears to head off to the right. Ignore this; instead, cross the wall stile.

4. Turn right along the surfaced lane. This becomes

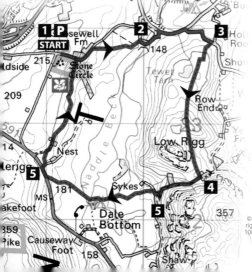

Dawn light: *The first rays of the rising sun catch Castlerigg's ancient standing stones*

a rough track that passes through a gate and then descends. When you reach an asphalt lane at the bottom of this drop, turn right and then immediately left through a kissing-gate just before the entrance to **Sykes Farm**.

5. The faint, grassy path heads to the right of the **rocky knoll** immediately in front of you and drops to another kissing-gate (west-south-west). Go through this and cross the next field in roughly the same direction to reach a gap between the fence and the wall in the field's far, right-hand corner. Go through the gap and make your way across damp ground to the **gated footbridge**. Cross this and continue west-south-west across the next field. Turn right on reaching a potentially soggy track—signposted A591. This ends just before reaching a gate.

Go through the gate and head gradually uphill with the fence/wall close by on your right. Cross an intervening wall via a stile about 40 metres in from the wall

Mists of time?: *Castlerigg Stone Circle half silhouetted against low morning cloud*

corner and then head straight across the next field to a gate in the top wall.

6. Turn right at the road and then right again along the track to **Low Nest Farm** —signposted 'Castlerigg Stone Circle'. Immediately after the cattle grid, go through the small gate on the left. Head uphill, following the line of the fence on your right. On reaching three gates, go through the middle one and turn right along the surfaced track.

Pass to the left of a **cottage** and then go through a large gate to the right of a converted barn. The path keeps close to the field boundary on your right and then goes through a small gate. Head straight across the next field (north-north-east) and go through a small gate in a drystone wall. Swing slightly left (north-north-west) to make for yet another small gate, beyond which you walk parallel with the wall up to your left. The faint path gradually eases its way up towards the fence on the left and then reaches the road. Turn left to return to **Castlerigg Stone Circle**.

If you haven't already visited it, go through one of the small gates on the left to enter the field in which the stone circle is

located. An interpretation panel near one of the gates explains the circle's history and shows a model of the stones as they are today. Just inside the eastern end of the circle is a group of 10 stones forming a rectangular enclosure known as 'The Sanctuary'. This mysterious feature is unique to Castlerigg. Excavations at the site have come up with few finds, although a stone axe head was unearthed in 1875. This is now in Keswick Museum. ♦

The second circle?

Castlerigg was first brought to the public's attention after it was visited by the antiquarian, Anglican clergyman and self-styled 'Druid' William Stukeley in 1725. His description of the stone circle forms the first written record of the site. It differs little from what can be seen today, although he claimed there was a second, even larger circle in a neighbouring field. However, no evidence has ever been found to back up this tantalising claim.

Moor Divock's atmospheric Bronze Age stone circle

Moor Divock stone sircle

An atmospheric walk across lonely moors dotted with mysterious Bronze Age remains

What to expect:
Quiet lane; tracks; open moorland, damp in places

Distance/time: 10km/ 6¼ miles. Allow 2¾-3 hours

Start: Village hall car park in Askham, about 6.5km south of Penrith

Grid ref: NY 513 237

Ordnance Survey Map: Explorer OL5 *The English Lakes North-eastern area. Penrith, Patterdale & Caldbeck*

After the walk: Queen's Head Inn, Askham, near Penrith, Cumbria, CA10 2PF. www.queensheadaskham.com | 01931 712225 | queensheadaskham@gmail.com

---

Walk outline

Leaving tranquil Askham, the route uses quiet lanes and tracks to reach the edge of the fells. Climbing gently on grassy paths, it makes its way on to Heughscar Hill for a superb view of Ullswater. It then drops to Moor Divock, visiting the Cockpit Stone Circle and other Bronze Age relics. The moors here are criss-crossed by trails and tracks, making route-finding potentially confusing. Compass directions have been included where there is a chance of going wrong.

The 'Cockpit'

Bronze Age remains

The climate was considerably warmer in the early to mid-Bronze Age, allowing people to move higher on to the fells. Consequently, many Bronze Age sites in Cumbria are located at about 150 to 350 metres above sea level. This is true of the moorland above Pooley Bridge and Askham, known generally as Moor Divock. Although only a few hut circles have been discovered here, there are many stone rows, stone circles and standing stones as well as at least twenty cairns, two of which have been found to contain cremations.

Bronze Age burial urn

The Walk

1. Leave the car park and turn right along the road. Take the next road on the left—signposted 'Celleron'.

2. About 1.5 kilometres along this narrow lane, take the vehicle track on the left—for **High Winder House and Cottages**. After a second cattle grid, the track swings right and then left. Ignore the track off to the right at this bend; simply continue uphill.

3. About 250 metres after the track swings left again, watch for a fingerpost. Turn right here and then go through the gate at a kink in the wall. Continue in the same direction for about 20 metres and you will reach some tyre tracks in the grass. Turn left here, heading uphill. The track is faint at first, but becomes clearer. Blencathra

soon appears to the north-west, but the best views are yet to come... Ignore another grassy track off to the left and then a narrower path (these are on either side of an underground reservoir).

With the ground dropping away, Ullswater appears. Inevitably, your eyes are drawn down the length of its dark waters to the mountains perfectly ranged around its south-western end—Helvellyn among them. It's a moment to savour.

The grassy track swings around the southern side of **Heughscar Hill** and descends to a wider track. Just before it reaches this clearer route, it splits.

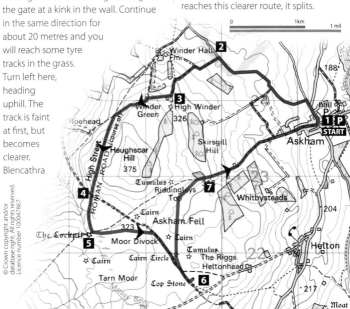

Mysterious: *The Cockpit stone circle with the North Pennines visible in the distance*

4. Bear right here to drop to a crossing of paths marked by a large cairn. Continue straight over (south-south-west).

5. About 500 metres beyond the cairned junction, you will see the **Cockpit stone circle** to the left of the track.

As with Castlerigg in Walk 1, no one knows for sure why the Cockpit Stone Cicrle was built. Constructed in the Bronze Age, it is about 30 metres in diameter with twenty-

seven standing or recumbent stones raised on the inside of a low bank. The tallest is almost a metre high. It is thought to have acquired its name in more recent history, when it was used for cock-fighting.

Take the stony path heading east from the stone circle, quickly veering east-north-east. After a particularly wet section, the path swings left. As it does so, cross the ditch on the right to pick up a grassy path heading east.

You soon pass through an area of large shakeholes known as the **Pulpit Holes**. These are formed when rainwater

Moor than meets the eye?: *Moor Divock stone circle sits in the midst of open moorland*

washes the sub-surface soil down into cracks in the underlying limestone. Eventually the ground collapses, leaving a small depression.

Turn right on reaching a broad, grassy track. You can see the **North Pennines** to the left, including **Cross Fell**, the highest point on the chain. After a few hundred metres, you will see a prominent standing stone to the left of the track. (If you reach the road, you've gone about 200 metres too far.) This is the **Cop Stone**.

6. Retrace your steps, to where a narrower track crosses the one you are on. You then pass an area of sunken ground on your right. Immediately after this, take the narrow path on the right that heads straight for an unusual **circle of stones** embedded in a bank of earth: more evidence of Bronze Age activity.

There are paths going off in several directions from here; the one you want goes north. Whenever it splits, or you lose it in the heather, keep heading north. About 250 metres beyond the stones, you come to a grassy track. Turn left and then, almost immediately, right to resume your northerly line. This track

eventually swings north-east. As it does so, ignore any routes off to the left.

7. The track ends at a gate close to the woods at **Riddingleys Top**. Go through this and walk downhill beside a wall.

Stay with the wall to pick up a clear track to a cattle grid on the edge of **Askham**. Follow the lane into the village and turn left opposite Askham Stores. The car park is on your right. ♦

The Cop Stone

This solitary lump of rock is another Moor Divock riddle. Almost 1.5 metres tall and 1 metre thick, the Cop Stone may have formed part of a man-made bank or ring cairn about 20 metres in diameter. Records from the late 19th century suggest there were previously more than ten stones around its perimeter. Yet, other theories claim the Cop Stone is a monolith that has always stood alone.

The tumbled ramparts of Carrock Fell's Iron Age hillfort

Carrock Fell hillfort

An atmospheric visit to an Iron Age hillfort and two summits linked by a lonely moorland ridge

What to expect:
Open grassy fell, faint paths and trods, boggy ground

Distance/time: 9km/ 5½ miles. Allow 3¼-3¾ hours
Start: Where the minor road along the eastern base of the Northern Fells fords Carrock Beck—about 4km south of Hesket Newmarket. Park on the grass just south of the ford.
Grid ref: NY 349 350
Ordnance Survey Map: Explorer OL5 *The English Lakes Northeastern area. Penrith, Patterdale & Caldbeck*
After the walk: Old Crown pub, Hesket Newmarket, Cumbria, CA7 8JG. www.theoldcrownpub.co.uk | 016974 78066 | stephenandbeverley.theoldcrown@aol.co.uk

Walk outline

There's a steep climb to Carrock Fell's 661 metre summit, but once you've got that minor difficulty out of the way, you're in for a treat. The wide, open spaces of the Northern Fells greet you, promising miles of superb walking. The route heads west from the summit on to High Pike (658 metres) and then descends via West Fell. The walk is almost entirely on grass, apart from the rocky summit of Carrock Fell itself and the peaty ridge leading to Miton Hill.

Pollinating the heather

Carrock Fell hillfort

The hillfort on Carrock Fell may be Cumbria's largest, but little is known about it. It is thought to have been built by the *Brigantes*, the Celtic tribe that dominated northern England in pre-Roman times. It commanded an excellent vantage point over the surrounding countryside with particularly good views to the north and the east. Little of the fort still stands today, but it is possible to get a sense of its size and shape from the remaining wall foundations.

Iron Age settlement

The Walk

1. From the ford, walk south along the road for about 60 metres and then strike off right (west) to pick up a wide, green path rising gently through the bracken. At the top of the first short rise, look to **Carrock Fell**'s northern slopes on your left. Cutting across this—heading north-east to south-west—is a faint path: this is your route on to the fells. For now though, keep walking parallel with the beck (west), crossing damp ground where the path becomes less distinct.

2. About 350 metres beyond the road, the path passes to the left of two small, grassy mounds. On drawing level with the second one, it swings left (south-south-west), briefly disappears and then begins climbing (south-south-west at first, veering south-west). When the path forks, bear left (south-south-west). Finally, with a bouldery slope on your left, the gradient eases. You can see **Skiddaw** to the south-west now. Just before you reach the very top of the ridge, the path suddenly swings left (south-east, veering east) and climbs to the tall cairn marking the **summit of Carrock Fell**.

Although little remains of the hillfort, take some time to explore the kidney-shaped summit enclosure. There are signs of an old, moss-covered wall just to the south of the summit cairn. Further east along the ramparts are the walls of a three-roomed medieval shieling. The shepherds who built

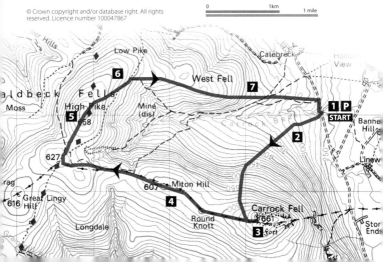

Water splash: *The ford and footbridge on Carrock Beck at the start of the walk*

this summer dwelling probably used stones from the old fort. Long before that though, it was the Romans who did the most thorough job of destroying the site.

3. From the summit, retrace your steps, but only for a few metres. As the faint path you came up on swings right, keep straight ahead (west) on a clearer path. At the bottom of the rocky slope, bear right at a faint fork to head west-north-west across the peaty plateau. The smooth, grassy 'bump' straight ahead is

Miton Hill. Should you lose the path as you cross the boggy areas, it is the hill you want to aim for. Yet, it's so small that, as you near it, you are barely aware of having climbed at all. The biggest clue to its existence is the tiny cairn marking the **top of Miton Hill**.

4. Beyond the cairn, you follow a much improved, grassy path across the open, expansive moorland. This drops into a dip. Keep straight on, climbing gently again now. Ignoring any trails to the left, stick to the path as it curves round the valley head and makes directly for High

Winter light: *The tumbled ramparts and modern cairn on the summit of Carrock Fell*

Pike. Cross straight over a wide gravel track and continue to the summit.

5. The **top of High Pike** is adorned by a bench, trig pillar and cairn-cum-shelter. The views to the north—across the Solway to the Scottish hills—are superb. From the trig pillar, head north to the **ruined hut** that now serves as a roofless shelter. From here, head roughly north-east along a fairly wide, grassy path. About 200 metres beyond the ruined hut, turn right (east). This path drops to a rough track close to some **mine workings**.

6. Turn left along the track and, almost immediately, turn right along a faint path (north-east, quickly veering east). Ignore the narrow path to the left; simply keep to this broad, grassy path as it contours the southern side of **West Hill**.

7. As you begin descending more steeply, you will see a mess of paths below. The **ford**, where the walk started, is east-south-east of your current location so, if you get lost in the maze below, keep this in mind. About half-way down the slope, take a narrow path on the right (south-east). This passes to the right of the remains of a **drystone**

enclosure. After crossing a faint, ditch-like track, the path swings slightly right and then crosses another grassy track before reaching a T-junction. Turn left along this clear, grassy track (east-north-east), but then bear right at a fork (east-south-east). Cross one more grassy track and then drop on to a broader, stonier track. Turn left along this. Turn right at the road to return, in a few metres, to the **ford** to complete the walk. ♦

What the Dickens?

Probably the most famous ascent of Carrock Fell was by Charles Dickens and Wilkie Collins during a tour of Cumberland in 1857. The walk is described in The Lazy Tour of Two Idle Apprentices, *co-written by the pair, although why they chose this fell remains a mystery. On the day in question, 'the sides of Carrock looked fearfully steep... the top... was hidden in mist', and Collins sprained his ankle.*

The Roman foundations of Hardknott Fort are still clear on the ground

Hardknott Roman fort

A fascinating visit to a dramatic Roman fort followed by an ascent of a superb little fell overlooking the site

What to expect:
Open grassy fell, indistinct paths, bouldery summit, some road walking

Distance/time: 7km/ 4¼ miles. Allow 3-3½ hours

Start: Roadside parking just east of the cattle grid at the bottom of Hardknott Pass, about 4km east of Boot, Eskdale

Grid ref: NY 213 011

Ordnance Survey Map: Explorer OL7 *The English Lakes South-eastern area, Windermere, Kendal & Silverdale*

After the walk: Woolpack Inn, Hardknott Pass, near Boot, Eskdale, Cumbria, CA19 1TH. www.woolpack.co.uk | 01946 723230 | office@greendoor.me

Walk outline

The walk first visits the Lake District's most spectacularly located Roman remains: the substantial walls of Hardknott Fort sit high up on a grassy spur above Eskdale with views across to the Scafell range. Those views—and more besides —dominate much of the walk as you then head up towards Hardknott Pass and climb to the summit of Harter Fell (653 metres). The ascent is mostly on grass, but the steeper descent negotiates slightly rougher ground.

Hardknott Roman fort

Hardknott Fort, often referred to on maps as Hardknott Castle, was built in the early part of the second century by the Emperor Hadrian. It housed 500 infantry soldiers from what are now Croatia, Bosnia-Herzegovina and Montenegro. Living in wooden barracks and leather tents at almost 250 metres above sea level, these men from the relatively warm Balkans had the unenviable task of guarding the high, wind-swept road across Hardknott Pass from attack by the Scots and warlike *Brigantes*. The fort was only abandoned about a century later.

Roman wall

Roman gold 'aureus'

The Walk

1. From the parking area, turn right and walk up the road for about 300 metres. Turn left at a squat fingerpost, ascending the path to the south-west gate of **Hardknott Fort**.

Passing through the gate, you can't fail to be impressed by the thickness of these walls, now nearly 1,900 years old. Some of the structures have been partly rebuilt from fallen masonry. These include the commandant's house, headquarters, a pair of granaries and external bath house, which lies to the south-east of the walls.

2. Continuing with the walk, leave through the north-east gate. (You'll see it directly opposite where you entered.) A faint, grassy path heads north-east, directly towards **Border End**'s crags.

It climbs slightly and then crosses a flat, grassy area—the Romans' parade ground. After climbing slightly from the parade ground, bear right along a narrow path (east-south-east), aiming for a grassy gap between the crags to the left and a small, grass-topped 'bump' to the right. On reaching the gap, continue on a faint trail along the base of the fell. This rejoins the road at a sharp bend. Turn left and walk uphill on the asphalt.

3. Having walked along the road for about 300 metres, turn right at a public bridleway fingerpost. Bear right at the next fork. You will soon see a fence over to the right; the faint, grassy track meanders to a gate in this fence about 300 metres south of where you left the

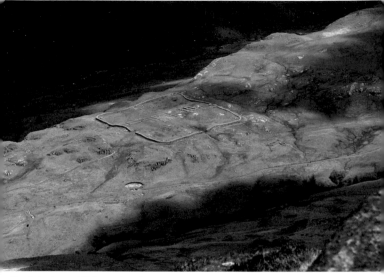

Cloud shadows: *A bird's-eye view of Hardknott Roman fort from Harter Fell*

road. Almost immediately after going through this, the grassy track swings sharp left. You will soon see another fence to your left. Follow the line of this fence, ignoring a small gate where the bridleway enters forestry land.

4. Crossing damp ground along the way, you reach a stile at a fence corner. Cross this and turn right. The faint path follows the line of the fence on your right at first, but then swings left. After leaving the security of the fence, it heads south-south-east for about 100 metres and then swings south-west to begin its grassy ascent of **Harter Fell**. It's not a well-used path, so you may lose sight of it at times; if this happens, simply head south-west to reach the summit.

As you climb, take time to turn around and savour the ever-improving views of the Scafell range and the other magnificent mountains at the head of Eskdale.

Don't be fooled into thinking Harter Fell is the dome of rock you can see straight ahead as you briefly follow a small beck upstream; that's **Demming Crag**.

Roman in the gloaming?: *Hardknott Roman Fort overlooks Eskdale*

5. The **summit of Harter Fell** consists of jagged crags and rocky outcrops.

The views from here on a clear day are simply stunning. The Lake District's highest mountains dominate the scene to the north and, out to the west, is the Isle of Man. Looking down on to the Hardknott Pass road, you also get an impressive bird's-eye view of the fort, putting its size and strategic position into context. The road that it defended was an important link between Ravenglass (Glannaventa) and the fort at Ambleside (Galava).

Come back down from the trig pillar, take a few strides to the south, descend to the right and then quickly swing right along a clearer path (west). Your descent steepens as you pass a **cairn**. About 125 metres beyond the cairn, ignore a path heading left; keep to the cairned route (west-north-west). Eventually, towards the base of the fell, you will be joined by a path from the left. Continue downhill (north-west). At an area of grass and bracken, you will see a fence straight ahead. About 150 metres before reaching it, bear right at a fork.

6. Turn right along a clear track and then through a gate. Walk downhill

with the pyramid-like peak of **Bow Fell** dominating the head of Eskdale ahead. Having dropped back into the main valley, go through two gates in quick succession. Descend to cross **Hardknott** **Gill** via **Jubilee Bridge**. This is just below the parking area where the walk began. ♦

Bathtime at Hardknott

South-east of the fort walls are the remains of a bath house. As in all Roman constructions of this type, people would have passed through warm, hot and then cold baths. In the hot bath, a curved metal tool known as a strigil would have been used to scrape dirt from the body. Just outside the Hardknott bath house is a small circular room, probably used as a 'sauna'.

The tallest Norse cross in England

Gosforth Norse cross

A low-level stroll along tracks and farmland close to Wasdale, circling a village with a rich Norse heritage

What to expect:
Roads, good tracks, farm paths

Distance: 9km/ 5½ miles. Allow 2-2½ hours

Start: Main public car park in Gosforth

Grid ref: NY 067 035

Ordnance Survey Map: Explorer OL7 *The English Lakes South-eastern area, Windermere, Kendal & Silverdale*

After the walk: The Globe Inn, Gosforth, Seascale, Cumbria, CA20 1AL. | 01946 725235

Walk outline

Gosforth, standing guard at the entrance to Wasdale, is a pleasant village with a long history. This walk uses quiet roads, a riverside path and a good network of tracks and bridleways to explore the area. Despite the fact that the highest point is less than 200 metres above sea level, there are some surprisingly good and far-reaching views to be had—of the fells one minute, and of the coast the next.

Norse heritage

St Mary's Church in Gosforth contains several Norse artefacts, including the tallest and most important Norse cross in England. With its fine, intricate carvings still clearly visible, it is thought to have occupied the same spot since 940AD. The Norsemen who created it came to Cumbria, not directly from Scandinavia, but from settlements in Ireland and the Isle of Man established by earlier Vikings. The area's Norse heritage is today clearly evident from looking at any map of the Lake District: *fjell* is the Norse word for mountain; *tjorn* becomes tarn; and *bekkr*, beck.

Crucifixion detail

Viking helmet

The Walk

1. Turn left out of the car park and walk through the busy village. Ignore the turning on your right to **Santon Bridge** and **Eskdale** in a short while; simply keep to the main road. Before long, you will pass **St Mary's Church** on your left, home to a Norse cross, 'hogbacks' and much else besides.

The Gosforth Cross is probably the most important Norse cross in England, not only because of its height (more than four metres), but also because of the detail of its carvings. With a combination of old Norse, pagan symbols and Christian motifs, the cross is said to depict the victory of Christ over the heathen gods. Although weathered, these can still be clearly seen. Look for winged dragons, wolves, serpents,

battles, a rather Scandinavian-looking Mary Magdalene and, close to the bottom of the east side, the Crucifixion of Christ. The meaning of all these symbols was lost until the 1880s when a link was discovered with the Norse figure, Loki, found on a stone in the church at Kirkby Stephen in the Cumbrian Pennines. The son of giants, Loki has variously been described as the 'trickster god', a shape-shifter and the Norse equivalent of the Christian devil.

You eventually reach **Wellington** where you follow the main road round to the right, crossing the bridge over the **River Bleng** and continuing towards **Wasdale**. Having climbed for about 400 metres from the bridge, you will see a

Family home: *Park Nook, Gosforth—once the home of the 'Parkers of Cumberland'*

bench on the left, close to the brow of the hill.

2. About 150 metres beyond the bench, turn left along a rough lane—signposted Guards Lonning. With ever improving views of the mountains to the east, including Sca Fell, the track climbs steadily. The gradient eases as you pass **Guards End**, a home set about 100 metres back from the track. The next dwelling you come to is **Between Guards**.

3. About 100 metres beyond this, go through the large gate on your right—it has path markers on it. Cross the ladder stile in the wall on your right. There are no paths on the ground now, but you should turn left to head down the field with the wall on your left, soon crossing another ladder stile. Continue in the same direction for about 80 metres and then go through a small wooden gate. (It's hidden from view until the last moment.)

Walk down the field with the wall on your right. Immediately ahead now are **Whin Rigg** and **Illgill Head**. After the

Mountain view: *Whin Rigg, Illgill Head and the Wasdale fells appear on the horizon*

next gate, the faint, grassy track veers away from the wall slightly, making for the farm at **High Thistleton**. You pass through a gate in a wall and then a kissing-gate next to a larger gate just to the left of the buildings.

4. Head down through the farmyard, keeping close to the buildings on your right, and then leave via the access lane. Having swung round to the south-west, the views of the fells you have been enjoying up until now have been replaced by views over the Irish Sea.

5. The track eventually drops to the road. Cross straight over to pick up another track—signposted Bolton Head and Hall Bolton. When the main track swings right in a short while—towards the buildings at **Bolton Head**—keep left, crossing a stile beside a large gate to access a potentially muddy track. Having gone through a large gate, you reach a T-junction. Turn right along the wide track which soon crosses the **River Bleng** via **Hallbolton Bridge**. The track passes beneath the buildings at **Hall Bolton** and then swings right.

6. When you reach the road, turn right. After walking on the asphalt for 200

metres, just before the road crosses **Bleng Bridge**, go through the gate on your left to pick up a gorse-fringed riverside path. Crossing several stiles along the way, keep close to the water's edge until you reach the next bridge. Go through the gate over to your left and then turn left along the road. Bear left at the junction in **Gosforth**, and the car park where the walk started is now 250 metres ahead on the right. ♦

Hogbacks

Inside St Mary's Church are two 10th-century 'hogback' grave tops carved with battle scenes and a fusion of Christian and pagan symbols that is unique to places where Norse and Anglo-Saxon culture co-existed. The slabs are thought to have once covered the graves of Norse chieftains. Then, in the 12th century, they were used in the foundations of the church's north wall, only to be rediscovered during major renovations in 1896.

Shap Abbey's ruined central tower dominates the view

Shap Abbey

A walk through beautiful countryside with far-reaching views and the impressive remains of a medieval monastery

What to expect:
Indistinct farm paths, quiet lanes

Distance/time: 8km/ 5 miles. Allow 2-2½ hours

Start: Shap Abbey car park, next to Abbey Bridge

Grid ref: NY 547 153

Ordnance Survey Map: Explorer OL5 *The English Lakes North-eastern area. Penrith, Patterdale & Caldbeck*

After the walk: Bulls Head Inn, Shap, Penrith, Cumbria, CA10 3NG. http://bullsheadshap.wordpress.com | 01931 716678 | karen.leicester@btconnect.com

Walk outline

This walk starts from Shap Abbey and visits a tiny chapel in nearby Keld as well as remote farms, the isolated hamlet of Rosley and other secrets of the tranquil Lowther valley. In terms of distance covered and ascent involved, it's a fairly easy walk, but the rights-of-way are not well used so you'll need to keep your wits about you as you follow the route description.

Shap Abbey

Hidden from view in a secluded hollow beside the River Lowther is Shap Abbey, built in the late 12th century. For hundreds of years, it was the home of an obscure religious order known as the Premonstratensians or 'white canons'. The canons were from an order of monks that originated in northern France and who sought particularly isolated and lonely locations for their abbeys.

Today, a substantial amount of the west tower remains and visitors can also see the foundations of the living quarters and church. Entrance to the site, open all year, is free.

Column bases

Medieval monk

Iconic ruins: *The central tower and ruins at Shap Abbey*

The Walk

1. From the car park entrance, ignore the bridge on the right providing pedestrian access to **Shap Abbey**; instead turn left. After 40 metres you reach a junction: cross straight over and climb the embankment opposite. As you approach some water board markers, turn right, later crossing a stile next to a gate.

Keep the fence/wall on your right as you cross this field. Beyond the next stile, follow the wall on your left. Just beyond a small group of trees, cross the stile in this wall and turn right. At the wall corner, head slightly right of the line you have been following to reach another wall corner. Continue with the wall on your left. Cross a stile, entering a private garden. Keep close to the wall on your left and you soon reach the road.

2. Turn right and then, when the road forks, bear right to pass through **Keld**. The **chapel**, or chantry, is the first building on your left. A key is available from the cottage opposite. Beyond the hamlet, the lane crosses the **River Lowther**. Go straight over at a crossroads—signposted Tailbert.

The North Pennines, including Cross Fell, are visible in the distance to your right. Before long, you will also see the eastern fells ahead.

3. The road ends at **Tailbert Farm**. Immediately after passing the farmhouse, turn right—through a gate on the other side of a small patch of grass. (There are no waymarkers here.) Go through the gate on the other side

of a tiny parcel of land. Now walk with the fence on your left, following tiny **Tailbert Gill** downstream through a pretty little valley. After a gate, keep close to the fence on your left. Eventually, this becomes a wall. When the wall swings left, drop to the road immediately ahead.

4. Turn right, but then leave the road after about 40 metres—as you draw level with a 'passing place' sign on the right. Turn left here, aiming for a wooden stile. After crossing this, bear half-right to make towards the farm at **Rayside**. Go through the large gate to the right of the first building, and then through the wooden gate in the wall on your right. Look to your left and you will see a large gate to the right of the farmhouse. Go through this and head along the lane for about 50 metres. On drawing level with a power pole on the right, turn left and walk through the long grass

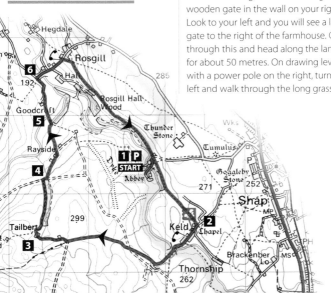

Roofless aisles: *Column bases, ruined walls and the central tower at Shap Abbey*

to cross a stile in a wall. With nothing on the ground to guide you, head north, weaving your way in and out of the tussocks. Eventually, you will see a wall on the far side of this field. About 60 metres to the right of a gap in this wall, you will find a small gate, hidden from view until the last moment. This provides access to the lovely old **Parish Crag Bridge**, over a beautiful, secret ravine on **Swindale Beck**.

5. Having crossed, walk beside the fence on your right. Just after passing

a farmhouse up to the left, the route crosses a tumbledown wall and continues with a wall on the right. The trail leads to a wall corner. Cross the awkward stile and continue alongside the wall. Go through the next gate and follow the wall on your left to the road.

6. Turn right to cross the **River Lowther** and head uphill through **Rosgill**. About 350 metres along the road, take the first signposted footpath on the right. This heads along a short driveway, passes to the left of a cottage and enters the back garden. Watch for a waymarker indicating your way out through a large gate to the left. Head south-east, go

through a gate and bear right, keeping close to the field boundary on the right as you pass through several fields. Soon after the third gate, you lose the guiding wall. Continue along the top of the embankment to reach a house. Cross the ladder stile to the left of this building and then follow the low fence on your right to the road. Turn right and return to the **abbey car park** to complete the walk. ♦

Keld 'chapel'

The so-called 'chapel' at Keld is thought to have been a 'chantry' owned by the Shap canons, dating from about 1350. The custom of saying Mass for those who had died became popular in the Middle Ages, some wealthy people even leaving money so that prayers could be said in perpetuity. Religious houses became overwhelmed by this practice, so they sometimes set up 'chantries' dedicated entirely to this purpose.

Kentmere's 13th-century defensive pele tower is now part of a farm.

Kentmere pele tower

An exploration of a remote valley that is home to a fortified farmhouse, a left-over from the border skirmishes

What to expect:
Quiet lanes, good tracks, some farm paths

Distance/time: 5.5km/ 3½ miles. Allow 1¾-2 hours

Start: St Cuthbert's Church, Kentmere. There is roadside parking for a few cars near the telephone box, just to the west of the church

Grid ref: NY 456 061

Ordnance Survey Map: Explorer OL 7 *The English Lakes South-western area. Coniston, Ulverston and Barrow-in-Furness*

After the walk: Wilf's Café, Mill Yard, Staveley, Kendal, Cumbria, LA8 9LR. www.wilfs-cafe.co.uk | 01539 822329 | info@wilfs-café.co.uk

Walk outline

This short walk explores a tranquil valley settlement via a series of delightful walled tracks and quiet lanes. It first pays a visit to the pele tower at Kentmere Hall before heading deeper into the valley. Following walled tracks that are a joy to walk, the route partly doubles back on itself to cross the River Kent and then continues upstream with ever improving views of the head of the valley. The return is via a little used lane.

Kentmere pele tower

Kentmere Hall, now a farmhouse, includes a 14th-century defensive tower with walls almost two metres thick. Known as pele towers, these structures can be found throughout Cumbria. They were built at a time when Scottish raiding parties were ransacking the region—towns were burned, churches destroyed and villagers slaughtered. Wealthy families built themselves these stout, sturdy refuges and, in the event of an attack, would move in—often accompanied by their cattle and other livestock. Kentmere Hall was the birthplace, in 1517, of Bernard Gilpin, a leading churchman in Tudor times.

'Brock Rock'

Highland cow

The Walk

1. From the porch of **St Cuthbert**'s, walk down the church path to the road. Cross the road and turn right along the track—signposted 'Kentmere Hall'. To see the pele tower at **Kentmere Hall**, continue to the end of the track. Having visited the farm, turn round and retrace your steps for about 50 metres.

2. Take the track on the left, heading uphill to the left of a wall. Go through the gate in this wall and cross the small enclosure diagonally, leaving via a gate in the top right-hand corner. Continue in roughly the same direction, through a gate to the right of a large boulder. Head to the right of the small building and pick up a rough track leading to some cottages.

The Brock Stone, or 'Badger Rock', near Kentmere Hall is a huge boulder left by the retreating ice sheet at the end of the last Ice Age.

3. Ignore the first track on the left—signposted 'Garburn Pass'. Just 80 metres on from it, take the next track on the left—signposted to 'Kentmere Reservoir'. Bear right at a fork and go through a metal gate. After about 300 metres, the track drops to a surfaced lane. Turn left.

4. Just before a cattle grid, turn right along a gently rising track—signposted 'Kentmere Church'. About 250 metres after going through a gate, turn left along another walled path. Drop to a farm track.

5. Turn left, passing to the right of the buildings at **Rook Howe**. About 200 metres beyond the farm—just before the track drops to a gate—go through a gap in the wall on your right.

6. Cross the bridge over the **River Kent** and take the trail straight ahead. Once

0   1km

½ mile

Medieval monument: *St Cuthbert's Church, Kentmere dates from the sixteenth century*

through a gap in a wall, turn left along the track (**Low Lane**). Immediately after a beck, bear left at a fork—signposted Mardale. Almost 400 metres beyond this fork, the track swings right. Ignore the path to the left here. Walk uphill, past a barn. The track swings left as it is joined by another from the right and then swings right again.

7. Turn right along the road (**High Lane**). Just over a kilometre later, take the next road on the right. At the T-junction, turn right. The **church** where the walk started is about 250 metres ahead on the right. ◆

Boar war?

Kentmere was given to Richard de Gilpin in the thirteenth century after he hunted down, fought with and killed a ferocious wild boar that had been plaguing the area between Kendal and Windermere. Many pilgrims on their way to holy sites near Kendal and Windermere had been attacked, and villagers went in fear of their lives. De Gilpin, descended from Normans, was also made a knight for his exploits.

A dramatic view across Derwent Water to Blencathra

Catbells mines

*Along the base of Catbells and back via a lakeshore path:
an area once busy with Elizabethan mines*

What to expect:
*Good tracks and paths,
lakeside and low fellside*

Distance/time: 7.5km/ 4½ miles. Allow 2-2½ hours

Start: Small parking area on Skelgill Road near Hawes End

Grid ref: NY 247 211

Ordnance Survey Map: Explorer OL 4 *The English Lakes North-western area. Keswick, Cockermouth & Wigton*

After the walk: Swinside Inn and Refuge Bar, Newlands Valley, Keswick, Cumbria, CA12 5UE. www.theswinsideinn.com | 017687 78253 | booking@swinsideinn.com

Walk outline

Using a lovely bridleway tucked away at the base of Catbells, the outward route heads south, as far as Manesty. The return route, weaving its way in and out of gorgeous woodland, uses a popular path along the shores of Derwent Water with superb views of Skiddaw. The climbs—none of which is particularly steep—are short and well spaced-out.

A mining landscape

Gazing across Derwent Water from Keswick at those seemingly perfect fells that form such a photogenic backdrop to the lake's western shore, it is hard to believe that, for centuries, miners tore into the heart of them for their mineral wealth: copper, lead, silver and even gold were among the riches to be found beneath Catbells, Maiden Moor and the other fells of the Newlands Valley. On closer investigation, walkers will discover spoil heaps, fenced shafts and even the occasional open adit. Organised mining in the area began in the sixteenth century and, in a few places, continued even into the twentieth century.

Derwent Water

Lead ore

The Walk

1. Take the path climbing from the eastern end of the parking area—signposted 'Catbells'. You will be joined by a path from the left. As it swings right, turn left to drop steeply to a broad path. Turn right here.

This delightful terrace path skirts the lower slopes of Catbells, never climbing above 200 metres, but always providing great views of Derwent Water and Borrowdale. After about 700 metres along this path, you come across the first signs of the old mine workings. The barren ground on the steep slopes above show where the spoil of Old Brandley mine was strewn across the fellside in the early quest for lead and silver. If you look towards the top of the ridge, you will see a fenced area—the holes left by the removal of the mineral vein here are about 50 metres deep, hence the fence. A little later on, as the path drops to the road, you will see more fenced workings. These are the remains of the Brandlehow Mine, which operated until 1892.

Minerals from mines in this area would have been taken to Brigham in Keswick where there were no fewer than six ore smelters.

At one point, the path descends to the road, but then continues almost immediately.

There are several benches on this part of the walk, including one that is dedicated to writer Sir Hugh Walpole. It overlooks his former home, Brackenburn, which he described as his "little paradise on Catbells". Walpole was born in New Zealand in 1884 and lived in Cumbria from 1924 until his death in 1941. He wrote a great deal while

Mirror-like: *A slight mist hangs over Derwent Water on a calm, frosty morning*

at Brackenburn, including his Cumberland family saga The Herries Chronicle, *which uses Watendlath as one of its key settings.*

2. About 2 kilometres after joining the bridleway, the route divides at a wall bordering an area of woodland. Keep left here, alongside the wall at first and then joining a wider path that drops to a gate. Go through this and quickly swing right to drop to the road at **Manesty**.

3. Walk along the asphalt for almost 300 metres and then turn left through a pedestrian gate to access a clear track—signposted 'Lodore'. After going through two more gates, the path divides. Bear left here. At the next fork, immediately after crossing a short section of boardwalk, bear right towards the lake. On reaching a T-junction a few metres back from the edge of **Derwent Water**, turn left.

Look to the right here and you will see a fenced area that hides a flooded mine shaft. On the lakeshore itself, the early miners would have chipped away at the

Lakeland beauty: *Looking across Derwent Water and its many islands to Keswick*

exposed bedrock by hand before the use of gunpowder.

Follow the well constructed track along the lakeshore and into the woods.

4. On reaching a rough lane at a slate bungalow called **The Warren**, turn right. Ignore the driveway on the right, but then, soon after the next gate, bear right at a fork. The path passes through a small gate close to the water's edge. The spoil heaps in this area are from **Brandlehow Mine**, which you saw from higher up the fell earlier. On re-entering the woods, bear right to stay on the lakeside path.

This is Brandlehow Park, the National Trust's first Lake District acquisition. It was bought by public subscription in 1902 to prevent housing development. Princess Louise, Queen Victoria's daughter, presided over the official opening. After the ceremony, she and the three National Trust founders—Hardwicke Rawnsley, Robert Hunter and Octavia Hill—each planted an oak tree.

As you leave the woods via another gate, you are faced with a choice of two wide, surfaced tracks. Take the one on the left and follow it to a metalled road.

5. Turn right along this lane, passing below the **Hawes End outdoor centre**. On drawing level with a private driveway on the right, turn left to climb beside a drystone wall—signposted 'Catbells and Newlands Valley'. Turn left at the road, soon crossing a cattle grid. Take the next road on your right, and the car park where the walk started is a little way ahead on the left. ♦

The German miners

In the sixteenth century, Derwent Isle in Derwent Water became home to a 200-strong community of German miners fleeing from the inhabitants of Keswick. They had been forced to leave the town after several of them were murdered. The Germans, at that time the best miners in Europe, were invited to England by Elizabeth I in 1564. They established copper and lead mines throughout Cumbria from their centre of operations in Keswick.

The bobbin mill at Stott Park has been restored by English Heritage

Stott Park Bobbin Mill

A wander through woodland and over rolling hills at the southern end of Windermere, once an industrial landscape

What to expect:
Woodland trails, low fell, long road section

Distance: 7.5km/ 4½ miles. Allow 2½-3 hours

Start: Lake District National Park pay and display car park at High Dam, near Finsthwaite

Grid ref: SD 368 882

Ordnance Survey Map: Explorer OL7 *The English Lakes South-eastern area, Windermere, Kendal & Silverdale*

After the walk: Lakeside Hotel, Windermere, Newby Bridge, Cumbria, LA12 8AT. www.lakesidehotel.co.uk | 01539 530001 | sales@lakesidehotel.co.uk

Walk outline

The walk climbs gently through oak woods to visit the small reservoir at High Dam. Clear paths complete a partial circuit of this serene body of water before the route heads across bracken-covered hillsides to enjoy great views from Stott Park Heights (190m). A steep descent through the trees and a walk along quiet, winding lanes to Lakeside is then followed by more woodland trails and field paths through Finsthwaite.

Stott Park Bobbin Mill

First powered by water and then by steam, the bobbin mill at Stott Park was built in 1835 to supply northern England's booming textile industry. Having been restored by English Heritage, the complicated mass of belts and Victorian machinery is in working order again, and, from April to October, visitors can watch bobbins being made.

The reservoir at High Dam was constructed to provide water to power the mill's huge waterwheel, while the surrounding oak woods would have been coppiced to supply wood for the bobbins.

Near High Dam

Bobbins

The Walk

1. From the car park, turn right along the clear track climbing gently through oak woods. Bear left at a fork to stay close to the beck. After a kissing-gate, keep left at another fork. You will soon see a small dam to the left. Do not cross this; instead continue uphill to a second **dam**, which you do cross.

2. On the other side of the dam, you pick up a good path around the southern edge of the **reservoir**. It's a pretty spot, surrounded by trees and with a couple of tiny islands in it. After crossing two bridges, the path goes through a gap in a wall. Keep straight ahead on a clear path (now a permissive route). A bench above the reservoir provides a pleasant place to sit and enjoy the view across to **Gummer's How**. The path then crosses flat ground on the northern side of the reservoir.

3. About 80 metres after a gap in a wall, take a faint trail to the left. This quickly goes through a kissing-gate. With improved views to the north, you begin losing height. Bear right at a fork. Go through a small gate to descend through the woods, soon fording a beck via a small concrete structure. Keep straight ahead through the trees for a few more metres, but then turn left along a clearer path.

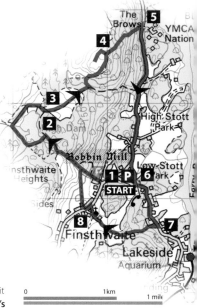

The path now winds its way gently uphill towards **Stott Park Heights**. Bear right at a fork and, within a few metres, you walk beside a wall on your right. This passes around the eastern side of the hill.

4. To reach the open summit of **Stott Park Heights**, turn left at the next path junction—close to an orienteering post. Then, at a faint fork, bear left to climb to the bench on the top.

High Dam: *Two dams were built to provide water to power the bobbin mill downstream*

You are quite some distance from the high fells at this southern extremity of the National Park, but the views are surprisingly extensive, covering the Coniston Fells, the Langdales, the eastern ranges and, of course, Windermere.

To continue, retrace your steps to the orienteering post and follow the path round to the left. This permissive route leads all the way to the road, following a rather winding, convoluted route that is, at times, concealed by leaf litter.

5. On reaching the road opposite the main entrance to the **YMCA**, turn right. This isn't a particularly busy road, but it is narrow, so please be careful. You will pass the entrance to the YMCA's **South Camp** on your left and, later, walk between the buildings of High Stott Park. Having walked along the asphalt for 1.5 kilometres, ignore a road turning on the right.

6. You soon pass the entrance to **Stott Park Bobbin Mill**. Ignore the next minor road on the right; simply follow the road round to the left.

Take a break: *The bench on Stott Park Heights is a great place to admire the views*

7. Just before the sign announcing that you are entering Lakeside, turn right along a clear, signposted path. This is immediately after **The Knoll** guesthouse. You now enter **Great Knott Wood**, which is managed by the Woodland Trust. Ignore a narrow trail off to the left near a beck. Climbing to a fork, bear right to reach a bench at the woodland edge. Cross the wall here and make your way through two fields towards the buildings of **Finsthwaite**. *The churchyard at Finsthwaite contains a grave that has become the source of*

much speculation over the years. The headstone is engraved with the name of Clementina Johannes Sobieski Douglass who died, aged 24, on May 16, 1771. She is said to have been the second illegitimate daughter of Bonnie Prince Charlie to his mistress Clementina Walkinshaw.

8. Go through a gate to join a surfaced lane. Ignore the lane up to the left near the **church**, but then turn left at the T-junction. Walk along the asphalt for about 35 metres and then turn right on to the driveway of **Plum Green cottage**. Follow the narrow path up to the left of a smaller building and out through a tiny gate. Bear half-right across the

field to a wall, and then walk with this on your left. After going through a small gate, the way ahead is unclear: pass to the immediate right of a caravan and then follow a faint, grassy track rising north. Enter the woods via a kissing-gate. Turn left immediately after the bridge to retrace your steps to the car park, remembering to bear right at the path junction to complete the walk. ♦

'Hard lives?'

There would once have been about 250 men and boys working at Stott Park, producing 250,000 bobbins each week. Bobbin-turning was a dangerous and unpleasant job with long hours. Children would have been used for jobs such as log-peeling—hand-stripping the bark from logs—for 12 hours a day, six days a week. They received no pay or education, just shelter and two meals a day.

Loughrigg Tarn with the Langdale Pikes behind

Loughrigg Tarn

A walk to one of the Lake District's most beautiful tarns, beloved of the Romantic poets and early tourists alike

What to expect:
Quiet lanes, good tracks, some farm paths

Distance/time: 4km/ 2½ miles. Allow 1¾-2 hours

Start: Roadside parking on the B5343 near the Skelwith Bridge Hotel

Grid ref: NY 344 034

Ordnance Survey Map: Explorer OL7 *The English Lakes South-eastern area, Windermere, Kendal & Silverdale*

After the walk: Talbot Bar, Skelwith Bridge Hotel, near Ambleside, Cumbria, LA22 9NJ. www.skelwithbridgehotel.co.uk/talbot-bar/ 01539 432115 | info@skelwithbridgehotel.co.uk

Walk outline

This short walk, starting from Skelwith Bridge, uses quiet lanes, grassy paths and pleasant tracks to visit Loughrigg Tarn. With the Langdales in the background, this is a wonderful place to visit with your camera—or just with a picnic. There are one or two fairly steep, albeit short, climbs involved, but these are rewarded with magnificent views.

Loughrigg Tarn

Inspired by the Romantic poets, aided by the birth of the railways and armed with early guidebooks, tourists began flocking to the Lake District during the 19th century, drawn to scenic locations such as Stockghyll Force, Buttermere and, of course, Loughrigg Tarn. This tiny body of water, sitting at an altitude of less than 100 metres, occupies an idyllic location that has the Langdale Pikes as its immaculate backdrop.

Wordsworth described it as a "most beautiful example" and gave it its nickname "Diana's looking glass" after the Italian Lake Nemi, said to be the mirror of Diana, the Roman warrior goddess of nature and fertility.

Yellow waterlily

Victorian tourist

The Walk

1. Starting from the junction of the B5343 Langdale road and the A593 in **Skelwith Bridge**, take the narrow lane heading steeply uphill to the right of some white cottages. After about 500 metres, turn right at a T-junction—signposted to 'Ambleside'.

2. After another 500 metres, turn left along a surfaced driveway in front of **Brunt How Cottage**. As it swings left, cross to a partly concealed fingerpost and go through the gate. A faint path climbs beside the fence on your right. Go through the gate at the top, turn right and then immediately left through another gate. The path continues uphill.

3. After a second tall gate, turn left along a clear path at the base of **Loughrigg Fell**. About 200 metres after this goes through a gate, watch for two gates close to each other on your right. Go through the second of these. Walking to the left of a **group of beech trees**, cross the small field and climb the stile on the other side. Walk briefly with the fence on your right before heading downhill.

4. Cross the stile, turn right along the lane and then cross another stile on the left. The route, unclear on the ground, passes around the north-east side of the tarn and then swings round its northern edge. After crossing a ladder stile, make your way up the grassy slope towards a gate. Cross the stile beside this and turn left along the quiet road.

5. Having walked along the asphalt for about 150 metres, turn right along a track—signposted Skelwith Bridge. This becomes a narrow path that enters the private grounds of **Neaum Crag** via a small gate.

0   1km

1 mile

Water margin: *The pretty path beside Loughrigg Tarn*

The path leads on to an asphalt lane heading down between wooden cabins. Go straight across at a junction and then swing slightly right across a gravel area between some more cabins. Follow the path through the trees and then back out into the open. Head straight down the grassy slope — in the general direction of the **Skelwith Bridge Hotel**. Once through the kissing-gate, you are back out on the **B5343**. The junction where the walk started is to your left, so completing the walk. ♦

The Picturesque

The idea of travelling simply for scenic pleasure started in the 18th century. Before that, mountains and the 'wild' were regarded as ugly things to be feared. It was the Cumberland artist William Gilpin who, inspired by landscape painters, first put forward 'principles of picturesque beauty'. Unusual at the time, he looked at the natural world and saw something aesthetically pleasing—an idea that resonates in tourism today.

Useful Information

Cumbria Tourism
Cumbria Tourism's official website covers everything from accommodation and even:
to attractions and adventure. **www.golakes.co.uk**

Lake District National Park
The Lake District National Park website also has information on things to see and do,
plus maps, webcams and news. **www.lakedistrict.gov.uk**

Tourist Information Centres
The main TICs provide free information on everything from accommodation and travel
to what's on and walking advice.

Ambleside	01539 432 582	tic@thehubofambleside.com
Bowness	01539 442 895	bownesstic@lake-district.gov.uk
Coniston	01539 441 533	mail@conistontic.org
Keswick	01768 772 645	keswicktic@lake-district.gov.uk
Penrith	01768 867 466	pen.tic@eden.gov.uk
Ullswater	01768 482 414	ullswatertic@lake-district.gov.uk
Windermere	01539 446 499	windermeretic@southlakeland.gov.uk

Local museums
To learn more about Cumbria's long and varied history, visit:

Tullie House Museum & Art Gallery, Castle Street, Carlisle, CA3 8TP
Cumbria's largest and arguably best museum. Fascinating history, geology, wildlife and
art collections. **www.tulliehouse.co.uk** | 01228 618718 | enquiries@tulliehouse.org

Penrith and Eden Museum, Robinson School, Penrith CA11 7PT
History, archaeology and wildlife collections, including the Newby Roman coin hoard.
www.eden.gov.uk/museum | 01768 865105 | museum@eden.gov.uk

Weather
Five day forecast for the Lake District: 0844 846 2444
www.lakedistrict.gov.uk/weatherline